DELEGATING FOR RESULTS—Revised Edition

By Robert B. Maddux

A FIFTY-MINUTE™ SERIES BOOK

CRISP PUBLICATIONS, INC.
Menlo Park, California

DELEGATING FOR RESULTS—
Revised Edition

Robert B. Maddux

CREDITS
Editor: **Tony Hicks**
Production: **Leslie Power**
Typesetting: **ExecuStaff**
Cover Design: **Carol Harris**
Artwork: **Ralph Mapson**

Copyright © 1990, 1998 by Crisp Publications, Inc.

Printed in the United States of America

Distribution to the U.S. Trade:

National Book Network, Inc.
4720 Boston Way
Lanham, MD 20706
1-800-462-6420

http://www.crisp-pub.com

Library of Congress Catalog Card Number 97-66609
Maddux, Robert B.
Delegating for Results
ISBN 1-56052-455-3

10 9 8 7 6 5 4 3 2 1

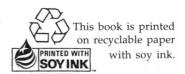

This book is printed on recyclable paper with soy ink.

LEARNING OBJECTIVES FOR:

DELEGATING FOR RESULTS

The objectives for *Delegating for Results* are listed below. They have been developed to guide you, the reader, to the core issues covered in this book.

Objectives

- ❑ 1) **To explain the delegation role of the manager**

- ❑ 2) **To show how to select and train employees for delegation**

- ❑ 3) **To point out potential delegation problems and how to address them**

Assessing Your Progress

In addition to the Learning Objectives, Crisp, Inc. has developed an **assessment** that covers the fundamental information presented in this book. A twenty-five item, multiple choice/true-false questionnaire allows the reader to evaluate his or her comprehension of the subject matter. An answer sheet with a summary matching the questions to the listed objectives is also available. To learn how to obtain a copy of this assessment please call: **1-800-442-7477** and ask to speak with a Customer Service Representative.

ABOUT THE AUTHOR

Robert Maddux is President of Maddux Associates, Consultants in Human Resource Management. He has consulted with many large corporations and small businesses over the past 20 years to enable the mutually effective utilization of people in a variety of work environments. He has worked extensively with organizations and people in transition and has been instrumental in facilitating the beginning of many new careers in business organizations and entrepreneurial ventures.

Mr. Maddux has designed and conducted management skills seminars in Canada, Europe, and throughout the United States and also has been a consultant in the production of a number of management training films. He has written many Discussion Leaders Guides for use in employee development and is the author of several best-selling management books, including *Team Building—An Exercise in Leadership; Building Teams for Your Small Business; Effective Performance Appraisals; Quality Interviewing; Successful Negotiation;* and *Delegating for Results.* He is also the co-author of *Job Performance and Chemical Dependency; Guide to Affirmative Action;* and *Ethics In Business.*

ABOUT THE SERIES

With over 200 titles in print, the acclaimed Crisp 50-Minute Series presents self-paced learning at its easiest and best. These comprehensive self-study books for business or personal use are filled with exercises, activities, assessments, and case studies that capture your interest and increase your understanding.

Other Crisp products, based on the 50-Minute books, are available in a variety of learning-style formats for both individual and group study, including audio, video, CD-ROM, and computer-based training.

PREFACE

One of the most difficult tasks for supervisors (especially new ones), is learning to apportion the work among the employees they supervise. The difficulty is often due to just those personal qualities—job knowledge, competent personal performance, initiative, motivation, and a reasonable degree of interpersonal skills—that made them successful employees in the first place and ultimately led to their promotion. Those qualities might lead new supervisors to believe they can do all the important work in their unit by themselves.

These qualities may have made the employee successful in the past, but they can become a heavy burden if they are misapplied in the supervisory role. The new supervisor must contrast the old assignment with the new and identify the critical differences. One of the most important differences is this: Since the new task is too much for one person to accomplish, other employees have been assigned to help. They bring skills and knowledge in varying degrees and expect to use them and develop them. So the supervisor is responsible not only for his or her performance but also for the performance and development of his or her subordinates. Their combined efforts are required to accomplish the goals and objectives of the unit.

The supervisor must recognize the role change from performing tasks to managing the performance of others. Concentration must now focus on planning, organizing, motivating, and controlling. This requires learning new skills and backing away from doing tasks that can be done by subordinates. The supervisor must learn to delegate and do it well.

If the skills of delegation are not learned and polished at every opportunity, success will be limited and the likelihood of promotion will be low. Those with limited delegation skills who are promoted will find their new jobs extremely difficult, and they will ultimately have a negative impact on the productivity of their unit.

Delegation is not some mysterious art available only to a chosen few. It is a basic management process that can be learned and honed to a fine edge by anyone who is willing to make the effort and able to get some practice. Providing the principles is what this book is about. Applying them is up to you. Good luck!

Robert B. Maddux

CONTENTS

P A R T

I

The Role of the Manager

MANAGEMENT IS A PROCESS

> Management is the process of working through individuals and groups to accomplish organizational goals and objectives.

When a person assumes a managerial position there is a distinct change in that person's relationships with other employees, and a whole new set of tasks begins to unfold. These tasks, taken together, are generally referred to as the management process.

Management practitioners and scholars vary widely in their definitions of the management process. These differences are usually nothing more than a choice of words. Some consolidate similar functions into broad categories; others prefer an extensive listing of individual functions.

The management process for our purposes consists of four primary functions: planning, organizing, motivating, and controlling. Good delegation, the subject of this book, requires skill in all four!

The next four pages will give you an opportunity to review your understanding of these functions.

PLANNING — Determining objectives and setting goals; drawing up plans that will implement these goals

ORGANIZING — Assessing resources (needed and available); scheduling work distribution; flowcharting

CONTROLLING — Setting standards and checkpoints for evaluating work against these standards; sampling the work flow; collecting feedback

MOTIVATING — Supervising the workers; training and developing them; giving orders; maintaining motivation and a productive work climate

PLANNING

Planning is the thinking that precedes doing. It is concerned with setting goals and objectives for an organizational unit and with preparing plans and schedules to accomplish them. In the list below, check those statements that you consider important elements in planning.

❑ 1. Interpreting goals and objectives passed down from above as the result of planning performed at a higher level.

❑ 2. Gathering the thoughts and ideas of the employees who are directly involved, as well as your own thoughts and ideas.

❑ 3. Formulating and issuing policies and procedures to accomplish goals and objectives.

❑ 4. Examining alternatives and selecting the activities and programs that will lead to successful results.

❑ 5. Establishing timetables and completion targets in keeping with priorities.

❑ 6. Determining standards of performance and how results will be measured.

❑ 7. Identifying the resources necessary for task accomplishment—people, time, money, material—and determining their availability.

If you are an effective planner, you checked all of the above.

ORGANIZING

Once planning is underway, organizing becomes essential. Resources—people, capital, equipment, raw materials, facilities—must be brought together in the most productive way to accomplish goals and objectives. In the list below, check the items that you think organizing should provide.

❏ 1. Appropriate staffing—the right number of people with the essential skills to perform the work that has to be done.

❏ 2. Delineation of responsibility and authority.

❏ 3. Alignment of major functions and structuring of the component parts into effective work units and teams.

❏ 4. Manuals, administrative guides, and other tools to make known how responsibility has been assigned and authority delegated.

❏ 5. A communications system for reporting and coordinating tasks between people and organizations.

❏ 6. Methods of problem solving and conflict resolution.

❏ 7. Facilities and equipment needed for task accomplishment.

If you checked all seven boxes, give yourself 100%!

REVIEW YOUR DELEGATION PRINCIPLES

MOTIVATING

Motivation, along with planning and organizing, plays an important part in the level of performance that will be achieved in any endeavor. To check your views on motivation, review the following statements and indicate which are true and which are false.

True   False

_____   _____   1. The needs and desires of employees have little bearing on motivation.

_____   _____   2. It is important to create an environment in which employees can meet their needs while meeting the needs of the organization.

_____   _____   3. Results generally improve when people are able to participate in deciding what the results should be.

_____   _____   4. Motivation to achieve results improves when employees are recognized for their contributions.

_____   _____   5. Studies have shown that communication has very little to do with motivation.

_____   _____   6. Coaching and training tend to raise personal levels of motivation.

_____   _____   7. Motivation to achieve results usually increases as employees are given authority to make decisions affecting those results.

_____   _____   8. Good supervisors pay close attention to the way employees respond when they assign work.

Statements 2, 3, 4, 6, 7, and 8 are true.

CONTROLLING

Controlling is concerned with results. It involves follow-up to compare results with plans and to make adjustments when results differ from expectations. In the following list of statements about controlling, identify those you believe to be true and those you believe to be false.

Controlling requires:

True   False

_____ _____ 1. Devising ways to assess whether goals, objectives, or standards have been met in a timely and cost-effective manner.

_____ _____ 2. Punishing employees who have missed their targets.

_____ _____ 3. Formulating methods by which the use of the various resources can be measured and evaluated for future planning purposes.

_____ _____ 4. Establishing systems that provide feedback at key points as the work progresses, so that deviations from plan can be identified, evaluated, and acted upon.

_____ _____ 5. Limiting employee authority to minor details.

_____ _____ 6. Reporting the status of activities and projects to those who need to know.

Statements 2 and 5 are false.

HOW WORK GETS DONE IN ORGANIZATIONS

Management is a leadership effort to integrate and effectively use a variety of resources to accomplish an objective. It applies to all organizations, whether they are businesses, hospitals, or political entities. Managers will do well to remember there is no one best way to plan, organize, motivate, or control. Each manager must continually increase his or her knowledge of management concepts and draw upon them until a winning combination is found that fits him or her, the people supervised, and the work involved.

One factor is central, however, to every management task. That factor is DELEGATION. The manager must know what is expected of his or her unit, when it is expected, and how best to employ his or her human resources to obtain the desired results. This means assigning work in a planned and thoughtful way.

> Delegation is giving people things to do. Management is accomplishing organizational goals by working through individuals and groups. It is easy to see that the two are closely entwined. And it is obvious that the manager who is not delegating is not managing.

Delegation, of all the skills and activities of a manager, is one of the most indispensable.

Case studies help provide understanding and knowledge you may not already possess. Several studies are included in this book. Please give each your careful attention.

The first case study (on the following page) will help you understand the importance of learning and applying the concepts presented in this book.

CASE STUDY 1

CASE STUDY 1

The Do-It-Yourself Manager

Joanne was a capable and enthusiastic professional. She was promoted to manage a group of five professionals doing work very similar to her own past assignment.

She began her new position thinking, "I was promoted because of my excellent performance in past assignments. Therefore, I must have greater expertise than any of my subordinates and can probably do most of the work better and faster than they can. I will train them when I have time, but right now I had better concentrate on getting the work out."

Joanne did not pass on any major assignments to her employees; she did the work herself. As time passed, her hours of work increased steadily and she was less and less available to her peers—and to her own supervisor, with whom coordination was important. Her employees were given only the most routine work, received no training, and actually knew very little about major projects in progress. One actually resigned because of the lack of challenge and personal growth. Joanne was too busy to replace him.

Finally, after 60 days, Joanne's supervisor called her in to discuss her performance. What would you have said to Joanne if you had been her supervisor? Summarize your comments below, then compare them with the author's on page 85.

_____

_____

_____

_____

_____

_____

TECHNICAL, HUMAN, AND CONCEPTUAL SKILLS

Many new supervisors and managers approach their jobs much like Joanne, and fall into the same trap. They do not see the difference between technical, human, and conceptual skills and how these skills apply to their position. Think of them this way.

DEFINITIONS		
Technical Skills	**Human Skills**	**Conceptual Skills**
Ability to use knowledge, methods, and equipment to perform specific tasks; acquired from experience and training.	Ability and judgment in working with people, including an understanding of motivation and leadership.	Ability to understand the complexities of the overall organization and where one's own unit fits into the total picture.

Lower-level supervisors need considerable technical skill because they are often required to train and develop new employees and technicians. At the other extreme, senior managers do not need to know how to perform all the specific tasks at the operational level, but they should understand how all the functions are interrelated. The common denominator that is crucial at all levels is human skill.

As supervisors move up in management they must learn to delegate jobs requiring technical skill to their subordinates, to give themselves time to learn the human and conceptual skills now required of them.

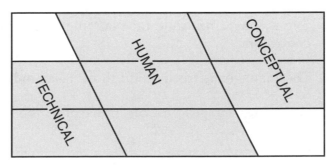

Top
Management

Middle
Management

Supervisory
Management

SKILLS NEEDED

WHAT CAN DELEGATING DO FOR ME?

New managers, like Joanne, often assign a low priority to delegation because they are unsure of how to go about it and don't see the benefits. Some actually think delegation is more trouble than it's worth. Some advantages of good delegation are listed below. Check those you would like to achieve.

- ❏ 1. More work can be accomplished and deadlines can be met more easily.

- ❏ 2. Employees become involved and committed.

- ❏ 3. The assignment of specific responsibility and authority makes control less difficult.

- ❏ 4. Employees grow and develop.

- ❏ 5. Human resources are utilized more fully and productivity improves.

- ❏ 6. Individual performance can be measured more accurately.

- ❏ 7. Compensation, including merit increases, can be more directly related to individual performance.

- ❏ 8. A diversity of products, operations, and people can be managed effectively.

- ❏ 9. Distant operations can be managed with less travel and stress.

- ❏ 10. Employee satisfaction and recognition are enhanced.

- ❏ 11. The manager has time for planning, organizing, motivating, and controlling.

- ❏ 12. The manager is freed to do those tasks only he or she can do.

Add any other advantages you can think of in the spaces below.

- ❏ 13. _____

- ❏ 14. _____

- ❏ 15. _____

II

Analyzing Personal Delegation Skills

HOW WELL DO I DELEGATE?

Here is an opportunity to learn how well you delegate. This scale will help identify your strengths and determine where improvement would be beneficial. Circle the number that best describes you. The higher the number, the more the statement describes you. When you have finished, total the numbers circled in the space provided.

1. Each of my employees knows what I expect of her or him. 7 6 5 4 3 2 1

2. I involve employees in goal setting, problem solving, and productivity-improvement activities. 7 6 5 4 3 2 1

3. I place my personal emphasis on planning, organizing, motivating, and controlling, rather than on doing tasks others could do. 7 6 5 4 3 2 1

4. When assigning work, I select the assignee thoughtfully. 7 6 5 4 3 2 1

5. When a problem occurs on a project I have delegated, I give the employee a reasonable chance to work it out for him- or herself. 7 6 5 4 3 2 1

6. When I delegate work to employees, I brief them fully on the details with which I am familiar. 7 6 5 4 3 2 1

7. I see delegation as one way to help employees develop their skills, and I assign work accordingly. 7 6 5 4 3 2 1

8. I support and help employees in emergencies, but I do not permit them to leave work for me to do. 7 6 5 4 3 2 1

9. When I assign work, I stress the results desired, not how to accomplish them. 7 6 5 4 3 2 1

10. When I delegate a project, I make sure everyone concerned knows who is in charge. 7 6 5 4 3 2 1

11. When delegating work, I balance authority with need and experience. 7 6 5 4 3 2 1

12. I hold my employees responsible for results. 7 6 5 4 3 2 1

TOTAL _____

A score between 72 and 84 suggests you are on target. A score between 48 and 71 indicates you are getting by, but could improve. Anything below 48 means you need to make changes.

SYMPTOMS OF POOR DELEGATION

There are many symptoms of poor delegation. They usually can be seen in the work habits of the manager, the attitude of the employees, or the productivity of the group. In the list below, check the symptoms that are visible in your organization.

❏ Deadlines are frequently missed.

❏ Some employees are much busier than others.

❏ The supervisor (me) is usually too busy to talk to employees.

❏ Employees are unsure of their authority.

❏ No one in the unit is ever ready for promotion.

❏ Employee decisions are often overruled.

❏ No one seems to know who is in charge of a project.

❏ The organization is plagued by slow decision making.

❏ The supervisor (me) never has time to visit employee work areas.

❏ Changes in plans and objectives are not passed on to employees with a need to know.

❏ Employees are assigned tasks they can't handle without training.

❏ The supervisor (me) sometimes intervenes in a project or assignment without informing the delegatee.

❏ Employees frequently request transfers to other units.

❏ The communications flow is sporadic, incomplete, and often too late.

❏ The supervisor (me) often takes work home and sometimes reschedules his or her vacation because of the work load.

❏ Talented employees are bored.

❏ The supervisor (me) insists that all mail must first pass through his or her office.

If you checked more than one or two of the above statements, you should look carefully at your delegation practices and ask yourself why these conditions exist.

COMMON BARRIERS TO DELEGATION

Ineffective delegators rationalize their inadequacies in various ways. They usually center around obstacles (natural or self-made) in themselves, in the characteristics of their employees, or in the situation itself. In the following list of attitudes, indicate those that affect your delegation practices by checking Yes. If they do not affect you, check No. Think about each statement carefully and be totally honest.

Yes	No	**SELF-IMPOSED OBSTACLES**
____	____	I prefer to perform operating tasks—not management functions—because I understand them better and I know how.
____	____	I can do the work in my unit better than anyone else.
____	____	I don't know how to delegate.
____	____	My employees won't like me if I expect too much of them.
____	____	I am not certain to whom I should delegate.
____	____	It is easier and quicker to do things myself.
____	____	We just can't afford to make any mistakes.

EMPLOYEE-IMPOSED OBSTACLES

____	____	My employees lack experience and competence.
____	____	My employees are already overloaded.
____	____	My employees resist responsibility.
____	____	My employees fear criticism and avoid risk.

SITUATION-IMPOSED OBSTACLES

____	____	Management expects me to handle the really important tasks personally.
____	____	My employees can't be trusted to work on their own.
____	____	We are seriously understaffed. I have no one to whom I can delegate.
____	____	Most of our decisions are made under crisis conditions.

If you answered "Yes" to any of the above, you will find this book most helpful.

FACT VERSUS FANCY

The statements on the preceding page to which you answered "Yes" need to be examined objectively. They usually are invalid and keep supervisors from delegating as they should. Several of them deserve close scrutiny.

The Fallacy of Omnipotence

This is the "I can do it better myself" syndrome. Even if it is true, the choice is not between the quality of the supervisor's work on a given task and that of the employee. The choice is between the benefits of the supervisor's performance on a single task and the benefits of spending his or her time in planning, organizing, motivating, controlling, and developing an effective team. The team will eventually outperform the manager and continue to grow.

The Fear of Being Disliked

Though few managers will admit it, most are concerned that their employees will dislike or resent them if they press them with a lot of work. Such a manager will risk personal burnout rather than inconvenience an employee.

Interestingly enough, employees rate supervisors who make full use of delegation as good or excellent. Poor delegators receive low ratings.

Lack of Confidence in Employees

Managers who lack confidence in their employees should look to themselves for the answer. They are, or should be, in control of the situation.

If employees cannot handle delegated assignments, the manager has either hired incompetent people, failed to provide them with appropriate training, or not made the effort to find out the extent of their capabilities. The remedy: Identify strengths and weaknesses, and train or replace those who still cannot meet standards.

Employees Expect the Answers from Me

This is usually how managers rationalize taking problem solving and decision making away from employees. It occurs when an employee brings a problem to a supervisor who says, "Why don't you leave it with me and I'll get back to you." When the supervisor does get back to the employee it is with the solution. The employee only wanted to talk about the problem—he or she didn't want the answer.

I Can Do It Faster Than I Can Explain It

A supervisor who uses this excuse to justify doing an operating task that he or she likes to do but someone else could be taught to do is making a serious mistake. If he or she doesn't take the time to teach someone else the task, he or she will still be performing it far into the future. This consumes valuable time and effort that could be better spent on tasks only the supervisor can do.

Sometimes a supervisor truly cannot delegate. But as the chart below demonstrates, upward progression requires more and more delegating and less "doing."

III

Preparing to Delegate

ANALYZE YOUR JOB

To become an effective delegator, you must have your own job well in hand. This means periodically:

- Reviewing your duties and responsibilities as a manager. How have they changed? What new things do you have to learn? How do they affect your unit? What are the new challenges? What old practices need to be stopped?

- Reaffirming the primary objectives of your unit. Have there been any changes that affect priorities or that need to be communicated to employees?

- Highlighting the key results areas. What are the make-or-break factors in your assignment? What are the areas in which specific results are essential?

- Reexamining your workload to identify those few tasks only you can do.

Remember, you are a manager, not an individual contributor. It is your job to utilize your human resources effectively to accomplish organizational goals. You must sort out the important from the unimportant and proceed on a priority basis. The more you develop your people, and the more you delegate to them, the more they can help you identify key results areas and meet objectives. Let go of tasks that rightfully belong to your employees. That includes troubleshooting and problem solving in their areas of responsibility. Be sure they are properly trained and help them when they flounder, but by all means give them a chance to do the job for which they were hired.

DECIDE WHAT TO DELEGATE

> Any time you perform a task someone else could do, you keep yourself from a task only *you* can do.

Managers usually delegate to give themselves more time to do complex and difficult management tasks, to improve productivity, or to develop their employees. Some types of work you should consider delegating are listed below.

DECISIONS YOU MAKE MOST FREQUENTLY.

Minor decisions and repetitive routines often consume a major portion of the day. Most, if not all, of these can be delegated by teaching employees the policies and procedures that apply. They probably already know the details better than you.

List two possibilities:

1. _____

2. _____

FUNCTIONS THAT ARE IN YOUR TECHNICAL OR FUNCTIONAL SPECIALTY.

These are usually operating tasks rather than management functions. You can teach others to do them. In fact, your challenge as a manager is to motivate others to produce better results than you ever did as an individual performer. Part of the time you save can be used to learn about other functions you supervise, so that you can manage them better.

List two possibilities:

1. _____

2. _____

TASKS AND PROJECTS FOR WHICH YOU ARE LEAST QUALIFIED.

It is almost certain that some of your employees are better qualified and can do parts of the job better than you. Let them.

List two possibilities:

1. _____

2. _____

FUNCTIONS YOU DISLIKE.

Performing functions we dislike is distasteful, and we often put them off or do them poorly. Examine the likes and dislikes of your staff as well as their talents. You will nearly always find someone who likes the job and can do it well. If that employee needs training, provide it.

List two possibilities:

1. _____

2. _____

WORK THAT WILL PROVIDE EXPERIENCE FOR EMPLOYEES.

This makes growth in the present job a reality and helps keep employees challenged and motivated.

List two possibilities:

1. _____

2. _____

ASSIGNMENTS THAT WILL ADD VARIETY TO ROUTINE WORK.

A change of pace is usually welcome and is often a good motivator for an employee whose job is growing dull.

List two possibilities:

1. _____

2. _____

DECIDE WHAT TO DELEGATE (continued)

ACTIVITIES THAT WILL MAKE A POSITION MORE COMPLETE.

As employees become more proficient, they often have time to spare. Add complementary duties and responsibilities to give their positions more substance.

List two possibilities:

1. _____

2. _____

TASKS THAT WILL INCREASE THE NUMBER OF PEOPLE WHO CAN PERFORM CRITICAL ASSIGNMENTS.

Maximize the strength of the group by giving people the experience needed to back one another up during emergencies or periods of unusually heavy work.

List two possibilities:

1. _____

2. _____

OPPORTUNITIES TO USE AND REINFORCE CREATIVE TALENTS.

Employees are not creative in a stifling environment. Stimulate them with difficult problems and projects, and reward creative solutions.

List two possibilities:

1. _____

2. _____

ASSIGNMENTS THAT WILL PROVIDE DIRECT EXPOSURE TO RELATED FUNCTIONS IN OTHER DEPARTMENTS.

Employees who perform related functions often learn from each other and come up with better ways to do the work.

List two possibilities:

1. _____

2. _____

TASKS THAT WILL BRING HIGH-POTENTIAL INDIVIDUALS IN CONTACT WITH MORE SENIOR MANAGEMENT.

This is a positive way for upper-level managers to develop an appreciation for the quality staff being developed within the organization.

List two possibilities:

1. _____

2. _____

Targeting Areas of Delegation

The following illustration summarizes what you have learned so far and may help you identify areas where you can delegate more.

- Others must do it.
- Others should do it, but you can help if necessary.
- You can do it, but others will if given the chance.
- You should do it, but others can help.
- Only you can do it.

Targeted Delegation

CASE STUDY 2

Baffled by the Budget

Jordan is an excellent manager of manufacturing, but he just learned in a per-formance review that he may have a fatal flaw. He is always over budget and his explanations are usually weak and late. This happens even though he prepares the budget himself and personally maintains what appear to be adequate controls. Now his supervisor has given him an ultimatum: "Get control of your budget or I will have to demote you to a less responsible position."

Jordan's administrative assistant, who has an excellent accounting back-ground, expertise with computers, and some experience with budgets, would like to help. So would his section heads, who believe the budget would be more representative of reality if they had some input. Jordan, however, feels it is his responsibility and he has to do it himself.

In the space below, outline what you would suggest that Jordan do to correct this obviously serious problem. Then check your answer with the author's suggestions on page 85.

MY SUGGESTIONS:

_____

_____

_____

_____

_____

_____

_____

_____

_____

PLANNING THE DELEGATION

Deciding what to delegate is only the first step in the delegation process. Delegation, like most other management tasks, is most successful when it's planned. It may take a few minutes for simple tasks, or a few hours when the project is complex. Your planning should include at least the following considerations. In the checklist below, check *Yes* if you include the item in your planning; check *No* if you do not.

Yes   No

___ ___ 1. What is the objective to be accomplished?

___ ___ 2. What are the critical completion dates?

___ ___ 3. What standards will have to be met?

___ ___ 4. What decisions will have to be made?

___ ___ 5. How much authority can I delegate?

___ ___ 6. How much authority will I delegate?

___ ___ 7. What instructions or orders will the delegatee(s) be authorized to issue?

___ ___ 8. Does a budget need to be developed or followed?

___ ___ 9. Who will the delegatee(s) need to interface with in my unit? In other units?

___ ___ 10. What information do I need to give?

___ ___ 11. How much do I want to be involved?

___ ___ 12. What feedback do I want and when do I want it?

___ ___ 13. Who will need to be kept informed of progress?

___ ___ 14. Do I need to tell others who is in charge?

___ ___ 15. To whom should I delegate?

If you checked *No* for any of the above items, plan on changing your delegation behavior so that you can check them *Yes* in the future. This checklist and the planning sheets that follow will help you more effectively plan your next delegation.

TASK/PROJECT

Key Results Areas	Results Expected	Critical Time Lines

ANALYSIS PLANNING SHEET

Standards to Be Met	Budget	Critical Interfaces	Frequency of Feedback

PART

IV

Selecting the
Right Person

MAKING CHOICES

As soon as you have completed your delegation plan, identify the appropriate person to perform the task. Some of the many things to consider are listed below.

DOES THE WORK BELONG TO A PARTICULAR POSITION?

Some tasks or projects fit right into existing work assignments and can logically be delegated there.

List two examples from the past or two possibilities for the future:

1. _____

2. _____

WHO HAS THE INTEREST AND/OR THE ABILITY?

Analyze employee job performance periodically, and keep an inventory of the interests and abilities of your staff. Look for opportunities to give employees who are attending classes a chance to apply what they are learning.

Give consideration to interest as well as to ability. A minimally qualified person may take the assignment enthusiastically and develop the required skills; the best-qualified person with a low level of interest may do a poor job.

List two examples from the past or two prospects for the future:

1. _____

2. _____

MAKING CHOICES (continued)

WHO WILL FIND THE WORK CHALLENGING?

Studies reflect that large numbers of employees are unchallenged, and their boredom is reflected in their performance. Give them the pleasure of a new opportunity to achieve.

List two prospects for the future:

1. _____

2. _____

WHOM WILL THE ASSIGNMENT STRETCH AND HELP TO GROW?

Some employees thrive on challenge and are willing to develop new skills to meet new job requirements. Give them the opportunity.

Identify two people in this category:

1. _____

2. _____

WHO HAS BEEN OVERLOOKED WHEN YOU HAVE DELEGATED IN THE PAST?

Delegate to all of your employees and stretch them when you can. Avoid playing favorites or over-burdening some of your staff.

Delegating to an employee who has been untested in the past requires careful planning, but the payoff in added performance is potentially high.

An assignment delegated with care can bring a problem employee up to standard. An employee with unused potential can be motivated to new heights of achievement.

Every time you give an "unknown" the chance to perform in a new way, the overall depth, versatility, and morale of your unit will improve.

List two possibilities for the future:

1. _____

2. _____

WHO HAS THE TIME?

If an employee has occasional periods with a light workload, look for opportunities to productively use that employee's time.

List two possibilities:

1. _____

2. _____

WHO IS BEING PREPARED FOR A NEW ASSIGNMENT OR PROMOTION?

Employees being prepared for a new assignment or promotion often profit from delegated assignments that relate to their new duties and responsibilities.

List two possibilities:

1. _____

2. _____

> **You really don't know what people can do until you give them a chance under the proper conditions.**

MAKING THE PREDELEGATION ASSESSMENT

The planning phase prior to assigning work is the manager's opportunity to organize the distribution of work and to schedule it within his or her unit. The quality of your preparations will largely determine the success of the delegation. Managers who ignore the planning are usually those who are keeping far too much work to themselves, or those who indiscriminately dump assignments on staff members. Asking yourself the following questions in advance will help you make better delegation decisions:

1. What work needs to be done?

2. What can and should be delegated?

3. What is the best match of work with individual employee abilities and interests?

4. Whom would the assignment help to develop?

5. Who can do it for me now?

6. Who can be trained to do it?

7. What is the employee's current workload and level of performance?

8. What is my best course of action, other than doing it myself, given the time constraints involved?

The checklist and charts on the next pages are a good place to summarize and record your thoughts.

REMEMBER YOUR SECRETARY'S POTENTIAL

Managers with secretaries, or administrative assistants, often fail to delegate properly to them. They see them only as someone to do word processing, answer the telephones, and keep up the files. This is a major mistake.

When secretaries have been properly trained and participate actively in the management of their supervisor's business affairs, they can be of incalculable value in a number of areas. Consider the following possibilities. As you do, check the tasks you already delegate to your secretary or administrative assistant, and be alert to new ways to enrich his or her job and facilitate your own.

❏   1. Screening and directing mail to the proper person for action.

❏   2. Composing correspondence for your signature.

❏   3. Organizing your time, coordinating appointments, and assuring deadlines are met.

❏   4. Following up on reports and other work on which you, or others, have set a due date, and reporting their status to you.

❏   5. Coordinating conference calls.

❏   6. Organizing and setting up meetings on your behalf.

❏   7. Gathering information needed for decision making.

❏   8. Maintaining appropriate personal records and files.

❏   9. Redirecting telephone calls and correspondence that come to you, but should go elsewhere.

❏ 10. Performing basic research on projects you have retained for yourself.

❏ 11. Maintaining confidential records.

❏ 12. Facilitating communication through your office in your absence.

Add other possibilities that fit your situation:

❏ 13. _____

❏ 14. _____

❏ 15. _____

DELEGATION

Key Results Areas	Results Expected	Who Can Do It for Me Now?

LOG

Who Can Be Trained to Do It?	Assigned To	Follow-Up Required

CASE STUDY 3

Making Choices

Olivia has been in her new managerial assignment for approximately two months. She is trying to make the transition from being an outstanding individual performer to being an effective manager. Delegation is very difficult for her, but she is making a real effort to learn to do it well. She directs a group of eight.

Her supervisor asked her recently how she was doing with her delegation efforts. Olivia replied, "I think I am doing pretty well. I have learned that Mary Wong is very knowledgeable about all aspects of the work, and she always completes the assignments I give her on time—even if she has to work overtime and on the weekends. So I give her all the big jobs and let the others stick to the routines they know best. My other employees just aren't qualified to carry the burden that Mary does."

If you were Olivia's supervisor, how would you respond?

_____

_____

_____

_____

_____

_____

_____

_____

_____

_____

Check your answer with the author's on page 86.

P A R T

V

Making the
Delegation

COMMUNICATING THE DELEGATION

> The heart of the delegation process is the interaction between the supervisor and the employee when the assignment is made.

This face-to-face, two-way discussion is the critical step that should end with employee commitment and the supervisor's assurance that the results needed will be achieved.

Delegation is not just pushing work down. When you are delegating, you are consulting and developing as well as assigning work. Open communication is vital, and success depends ultimately on the communication skills of the manager and the employee and on the quality of their relationship. When there is a lack of trust on either side, or poor communication between them, the needed understanding and motivation are unlikely to be there.

The following steps are essential in communicating an assignment:

1. DESCRIBE AS FULLY AS POSSIBLE THE PROJECT OR TASK AND THE RESULTS EXPECTED.

   Pass on all the information needed to get the job started, or let the employee know where it can be obtained. Indicate who else will be involved and describe their roles.

2. AGREE ON STANDARDS OF PERFORMANCE AND TIMETABLES.

   The scope of the assignment has already been determined, but you will want the employee's input on standards and a reasonable timetable for completion of the assignment.

3. DETERMINE ANY TRAINING OR SPECIAL HELP THAT WILL BE NEEDED, AND WHEN IT WILL BE PROVIDED.

COMMUNICATING THE DELEGATION
(continued)

4. DEFINE PARAMETERS AND THE RESOURCES, INCLUDING BUDGET, THAT WILL BE AVAILABLE.

5. STATE THE AMOUNT AND FREQUENCY OF FEEDBACK YOU EXPECT.

6. SPELL OUT THE AMOUNT OF AUTHORITY BEING DELEGATED.

   This should be balanced according to the complexity of the task, your confidence in the employee, and your need to keep others informed.

   See page 49 to select an appropriate level.

7. TELL OTHERS WHO IS IN CHARGE.

   It is important that you do not become a communications block between the delegatee and others who will be involved or affected.

It is easy to see from these seven basic points that delegation is *not* more trouble than it's worth. Have you been missing some good opportunities because you thought it was?

MISSED OPPORTUNITIES

Supervisors who find themselves deeply involved in the detailed work of their units sometimes wake up to the fact that the job is controlling them. They are controlling nothing. If they examine the situation carefully (while pondering the fact that their employees went home hours ago and they are still working), they often see the reason for their plight. Their reaction is usually, "If I had delegated this to Clifford or Sue in the first place, I wouldn't be having this problem now."

How many times have you missed the opportunity to delegate, or thought you had, and found yourself doing work someone else could and should have done?

By now, some missed opportunities to delegate have no doubt come to mind. List them in the space provided below . . . and resolve not to let it happen again.

MY MISSED OPPORTUNITIES

_____

_____

_____

_____

_____

_____

_____

_____

_____

_____

_____

SIX LEVELS OF AUTHORITY

A common management mistake is failing to delegate the right amount of authority considering the task, the surrounding circumstances, and the employee's ability. Some managers do not delegate any authority because they want full personal control. Others give full authority because they want to be free of the task. Most of the time, something in between these two extremes is called for. Before you make your next delegation, review the delegation levels described on the next page and select the one that fits your needs.

THE DO-IT-YOURSELF MANAGER
WHO HATES TO GIVE UP CONTROL

SIX LEVELS OF DELEGATION

Level of Authority	Assignment	Reason
1	Look into the situation. Get all the facts and report them to me. I'll decide what to do.	The employee is new to the job and the supervisor wants to retain control of the outcome.
2	Identify the problem. Determine alternative solutions and the pluses and minuses of each. Recommend one for my approval.	The employee is being developed and the supervisor wants to see how he or she approaches problems and makes decisions.
3	Examine the issues. Let me know what you intend to do, but don't take action until you check with me.	The supervisor has confidence in the employee, but does not want action taken without his or her approval. This may be because of constraints from higher management, or the need to communicate the action to others before it is taken.
4	Solve the problem. Let me know what you intend to do, then do it, unless I say not to.	The supervisor has respect for the employee's ability and judgment, and only wants a final check before action is taken.
5	Take action on this matter, and let me know what you did.	The supervisor has full confidence in the employee and has no need to be consulted before action is taken. He or she wants to know the outcome.
6	Take action. No further contact with me is necessary.	The supervisor has total confidence in the employee. The employee has full authority to act and does not need to report the results back to the supervisor.

FOLLOWING-THROUGH

> The goal in delegation is satisfactory completion of the assigned task or project through the personal efforts of those handling the task or project.

It is important, however, that the manager follow through with any support, resources, or information promised. It is also important that a feedback mechanism, suitable to the situation, be established between the delegatee and the manager. These considerations are all part of the preparations for delegation, and should be covered when the delegation is made.

THE ESSENTIAL ELEMENTS OF FOLLOW-THROUGH		
The Manager's Role	**The Manager's Communication**	**The Manager's Action**
Encourage independence.	Share all pertinent information.	Assess results.
Allow freedom of action in keeping with the level of delegation.	Do not become a communications block between the employee and the others involved.	Suggest course corrections if appropriate and unrecognized by those handling tasks.
Support initiative and creativity.	Monitor progress, but do not hover.	Help solve problems, but only those that are beyond the employee's ability to handle.
Share opinions and show interest.	Provide honest feedback.	Evaluate performance.
Accept mistakes and learn from them.	Insist that your need to know be fulfilled on time.	Plan any needed training for the future.
Provide training when needed.		Compliment efforts and reward success.
Live with differences as long as objectives are met.		
Be available.		
Don't take the job back unless absolutely essential (coach through problems).		

CASE STUDY 4

The Incomplete Data Dilemma

Marla is the manager of an insurance company claims group. Her employees are well trained and have considerable experience in claims work. Much of the work is routine, but occasionally an unusual claim is submitted that requires a great deal of investigation. When this occurs, Marla assigns one of her claims representatives to the case. She delegates the authority necessary for that person to gather the facts, develop alternative solutions, and recommend the action to be taken. Something always seems to go wrong, however. Key information is lacking or has not been considered. This is true even though Marla often acts as the point of contact when people outside the company are providing pertinent data. She always tries to pass this information on quickly and in a form that those handling the assignment will understand.

She has had several discussions with her staff about this, but the discussions only make them angry and defensive.

What do you think the problem is? Jot down your ideas in the space below.

_____

_____

_____

_____

_____

_____

_____

_____

_____

Turn to page 86 and check your ideas with those of the author.

P A R T

VI

Preparing Employees
for Delegation

WHAT YOU SHOULD EXPECT

The manager has every right to expect results from the employee according to the parameters established when the delegation was made. Check the expectations you feel are currently being satisfied when you delegate:

❑ 1. The employee has a willing, can-do attitude and accepts responsibility for the task.

❑ 2. The employee asks questions and seeks help when needed.

❑ 3. Progress reports are furnished on time to you and to others in the communications loop.

❑ 4. The finished tasks are good examples of completed staff work.

❑ 5. The employee uses initiative and shows dedication and commitment to the task.

❑ 6. Time, money, equipment, and worker hours are seen as expensive resources and used accordingly.

If these expectations are to be met, the employee must be prepared in advance, permitted to grow as the work is done, and continuously developed for heavier assignments in the future.

PREPARATION BEGINS WITH EMPLOYMENT

If a manager is to have a strong team to whom he or she can delegate, team members must be hired with that thought in mind. Human resources are the most critical part of any manager's success. Good people help ensure profitability, productivity, growth, and long-term survival. Some critical elements in employee selection and placement are listed below. Indicate how well you perform by checking the appropriate box.

	Do Well	Should Improve
1. I analyze job requirements thoroughly before beginning the selection process.	❏	❏
2. I always probe for objective evidence of a candidate's skills; knowledge; past successes and failures; dependability; and attitude toward work, co-workers, supervisors, and customers.	❏	❏
3. I determine the type of project and task responsibility the applicant has had in previous positions, and how he or she has handled authority.	❏	❏
4. I make sure each applicant understands the job requirements and expected standards of performance.	❏	❏
5. I describe my idea of teamwork to applicants and ask them to assess how they would work under team conditions.	❏	❏
6. In making a selection decision, I evaluate facts carefully and avoid coming to premature conclusions or stereotyping.	❏	❏
7. People I hire are placed in positions where there is potential for success.	❏	❏

> If the people you select to be on your team are successful, you will be successful.

DEVELOP EMPLOYEES TO HANDLE COMPLEX TASKS

Do you use delegation to build new employee skills and strengthen existing ones? Do you prepare people properly for assignments you wish to delegate to them? Your attitude, knowledge, and approach will influence what is learned and how well it is applied. Here are some suggestions to improve the return on investment in training for all concerned.

Place a ✔ in the box if you already do what is suggested. Place an X in the box if you plan to begin this practice.

I normally:

❑ 1. Review performance against expectations with each employee, and jointly we identify training that will strengthen results.

❑ 2. Listen to employees' growth objectives and support them through delegation when I can.

❑ 3. Talk in advance to employees selected for training, to emphasize the importance of the training to their job and their delegated assignments.

❑ 4. Have an employee's work covered by others while that employee is in formal training, so that he or she can concentrate on what is being taught.

❑ 5. Help employees develop an action plan to apply their training to the job and to any additional assignments I delegate.

❑ 6. Ask the employees for an evaluation of the training program and whether it would be suitable for other members of the team.

❑ 7. Delegate work to employees that allows them to apply new techniques and methods learned during training.

❑ 8. Compliment employees when they apply their newly acquired skills.

Qualified employees are receptive to delegation and the growth opportunities it provides.

TEACH EMPLOYEES PROBLEM-SOLVING TECHNIQUES

Many supervisors spend too much time solving problems that could be better handled by the employees they supervise. When supervisors try to solve all the problems, production is slowed, employees are frustrated, and personal growth is limited. The supervisor ends up with less time to plan, organize, motivate, and control. Delegation is more effective when the supervisor participates in problem solving only when necessary, instead of dominating it. In view of this, problem solving should be taught at every level of the organization.

The problem-solving process should be as simple as possible while getting the job done. One basic approach is outlined below. Check those steps that would be useful in your operation:

❏ **STEP 1—State what appears to be the problem.**
The real problem may not surface until facts have been gathered and analyzed. Therefore, start with a supposition that can later be confirmed or corrected.

❏ **STEP 2—Gather facts, feelings, and opinions.**
What happened? Where, when, and how did it occur? What is its size, scope, and severity? Who and what is affected? Is it likely to happen again? Does it need to be corrected? Time and expense may require problem solvers to think through what they need and assign priorities to the more critical elements.

❏ **STEP 3—Restate the problem.**
The facts help make this possible, and provide supporting data. The actual problem may or may not be the same as stated in Step 1.

❏ **STEP 4—Identify alternative solutions.**
Generate ideas. Do not eliminate any possible solutions until several have been discussed.

❏ **STEP 5—Evaluate alternatives.**
Which will provide the optimum solution? What are the risks? Are the costs in keeping with the benefits? Will the solution create new problems?

❏ **STEP 6—Implement the decision.**
Who must be involved? To what extent? How, when, and where? Whom will the decision impact? What might go wrong? How will results be reported and verified?

❏ **STEP 7—Evaluate the results.**
Test the solution against the desired results. Modify the solution if better results are needed.

MAKE EMPLOYEE COMMITMENT POSSIBLE

Managers cannot do it all, no matter how talented and committed they may be. Their success is measured by their ability to delegate intelligently and then motivate employees to accomplish the goals of the organization. The highest level of achievement is attained when a team is committed to the task and full use is made of each member's talents.

Commitment cannot be forced. It is self-generating and usually develops through a feeling of involvement. People increase their commitment to a team when they are allowed to contribute to its success. Once a person is actively involved in delegated projects and activities, including problem solving, a sense of ownership is developed. People feel more important and needed when they share a responsibility for results. Employees contribute their best to problem solving when they have a personal stake in doing so.

A manager controls the degree to which employees are involved. Open up opportunities for participation through delegation, and watch the commitment grow.

DIFFERENCES BETWEEN DELEGATORS

The manager's attitude toward employees and their ability to handle delegated assignments can make a significant difference. In the two lists below, check those items that best describe you.

Success-Centered Delegator	Doubt-Centered Delegator
❏ Concentrates on successful results and high goals.	❏ Focuses on and transmits fear of failure. Sets fail-safe goals.
❏ Reinforces employees' strengths and abilities. Confident of success.	❏ Expresses grave doubts about employees' abilities and limits, or arbitrarily reduces authority.
❏ Encourages employee participation in setting goals and objectives.	❏ Personally sets arbitrary goals and objectives.
❏ Readily accepts new ideas and creative solutions.	❏ Discourages anything new or untried.
❏ Communicates freely and openly. Nothing is held back.	❏ Withholds information to force employees to ask for help.
❏ Recognizes achievement and reinforces it.	❏ Doesn't recognize success until it is endorsed from above.
❏ Looks at the implications of each assignment for the future and assigns tasks accordingly.	❏ Focuses on short-range goals and discourages employees who see implications for the future.
❏ Encourages employees to appraise their performance and suggest improvements.	❏ Tells people what went wrong and what to do about it.

CASE STUDY 5

The Delegation Disaster

When Gino took over the systems group in the electronics division, he made up his mind to change the environment and hopefully the attitudes of the employees. His predecessor had not been an effective delegator or communicator. The employees had little to do in a department where the supervisor was totally swamped.

Gino immediately began to delegate assignments (at fairly high authority levels) that his predecessor had performed herself. He was surprised at the results.

His employees seemed to think he was pushing *his* work on them. Most of them complained they were neither trained nor paid to do the assignments delegated. It was not unusual for them to bring problems arising from their normal assignments to Gino for solutions, and they did not understand him saying, "Don't bring me problems, bring me solutions."

Has Gino overlooked anything in his approach to turning this situation around? Make your comments in the space below.

_____

_____

_____

_____

_____

_____

_____

_____

See page 87 for the author's comments.

VII

Potential Delegation Problems and How to Handle Them

DELEGATOR'S TROUBLESHOOTING GUIDE

Possible Problems	Possible Solutions
1. Supervisor delegates only meaningless chores.	Delegating only meaningless chores creates resentment. Mix in some of your favorite things and share the good times.
2. Employees resist the work, claiming they don't know how to do it.	Provide training as necessary, or break down the job and let them handle as many components as they can. Add more as they learn.
3. The employee says he or she is too busy.	If that is true, consider giving the task to someone else, but verify their workload first.
4. The task is repetitive, but it would take you longer to delegate the job than to do it yourself.	Get smart. At least have someone start to learn the process. Soon they will be doing it all. Otherwise you will still be doing it next year.
5. "Higher management requires me to sign these invoices and other basic documents like shipping and receiving papers."	Ask management to change the policy so that employees closer to the work can sign. You're probably already taking their word that it's all right to do so.
6. "Poor results on this project will make me look bad."	Your job is to let subordinates develop by taking on new endeavors. They may make some mistakes, but they will learn from them. You can minimize serious mistakes by using an appropriate level of delegation.
7. "If my employees can do the tough jobs well, I'm not needed."	Management desperately needs managers who can get superior performance from employees. Keep up the good work!

DELEGATOR'S TROUBLESHOOTING GUIDE (continued)

Possible Problems	Possible Solutions
8. "My supervisor expects me to do this personally."	If that is the actual case, you had better do it, but first check it out with the boss. She or he may just want to be sure you see that it gets done.
9. "I'll lose my skills if I delegate too much of the work."	Managers need to learn to manage. They need to teach their employees the skills needed for what they used to do.
10. "If I delegate all my work, I won't have anything to do."	Direct your attention to planning, organizing, motivating, and controlling.
11. "I don't understand the work well enough to control it or make a judgment about how well it is being done."	Learn enough about unfamiliar areas to ask the right questions and assess the answers.
12. Employees with delegated tasks keep coming back for advice and help.	Whenever an employee asks how you would do the task, turn it around and ask how she or he would do it. Reinforce correct answers warmly. If you feel sure she or he can handle the problem, or the consequences of an error are low, be unavailable. Help them build confidence.
13. Some employees are over-burdened and others don't have enough to do.	The supervisor is overdelegating to those who are most trusted, and failing to develop those in whom she or he lacks confidence. It is essential to balance the work and raise the confidence level by giving everyone a chance to perform.

Possible Problems	Possible Solutions
14. Employees do not understand organizational objectives and standards.	Tell the employees what is at stake and the why of the job. As often as you can, involve the employees in setting objectives and standards.
15. "Employees don't do things the way I do."	Concentrate on getting the right results and learn to live with differences. You may even learn something new.
16. The supervisor delegates either everything or nothing.	Study the levels of delegation described on page 49 and learn to apply them.
17. The supervisor assigns the least challenging work to the most qualified people.	Sometimes necessary, but often done because the supervisor fears mistakes. Select a level of delegation that fits the employee and the situation. Some mistakes will occur; they will provide learning experiences. It's a serious mistake to burn out your best people.
18. The supervisor and the employee have trouble agreeing on the specifics of the delegation.	Review and clarify objectives to be sure they are understood. Delegate accordingly. Don't be a nitpicker. Follow up as necessary to see that the right results are being obtained.
19. The employee's performance is jeopardizing a successful outcome.	Identify the reason and take corrective action. This might include changing the level of authority and providing more support. Acting carelessly could shatter the employee's confidence.
20. Deadlines are not being met.	Reassess objectives, standards, and priorities with the employee. Identify the reasons for missed deadlines and take corrective action.

VIII

Using Delegation as a Tool in Managing Change

CHANGE IS LEGITIMATE BUT REQUIRES SMOOTH TRANSITIONS

In some organizations the word "change" itself is enough to produce strong emotional reactions. There are those who fear it, those who misunderstand its purpose, and those who thrive on it.

Change is actually healthy and positive when it is well planned and when those who are affected by it are committed to the objectives it is designed to achieve. Under these circumstances change tends to stabilize conditions rather than upset them. It tends to keep the organization in touch with the changing realities of the world rather than on a comfortable road to disaster.

One of the key skills in management is introducing change and overcoming the resistance that may impede a smooth transition. Unfortunately, managers in recent years have been caught in a whirlpool of change that has often diminished their financial resources, reduced their staff, cut their training budget, and increased their personal workload. They have witnessed, and often presided over, the elimination of layers of management and support staff, which included many friends and trusted associates. Not all these changes have been well planned and in many cases chaos rather than efficiency has reigned. Transitions have been anything but smooth.

When transitional issues negatively impact productivity, profitability, and customer satisfaction, managers are expected to overcome obstacles and solve the problems. During such times, it is often possible to use delegation techniques to inform employees, permit direct participation in transitional activities, reduce anxieties, and focus their attention on meaningful goals.

> *The art of progress is to preserve order amid change and to preserve change amid order.*
>
> —Alfred North Whitehead

THE KEY ELEMENT IN CHANGE IS HUMAN

Using delegation to facilitate change requires an understanding of the initial impact change has on organizations and their people. A summary follows.

Changes occur for many reasons, including new technology, a need for new systems, or the belief that a change in the organization's structure will improve its efficiency or profitability. Unfortunately, management sometimes becomes so caught up in the mechanical aspects of such changes that they forget the most critical factor of all—the people affected.

The simple fact is that people resist change. Research suggests a number of reasons. Check those in the list below with which you are familiar.

❑ Fear of failure in a different environment.

❑ The objective of the change is not clear.

❑ Persons affected by the change are not involved in the planning.

❑ Communication about the change is poor.

❑ Anxiety over job security goes unrelieved.

❑ There is high satisfaction with the status quo.

❑ The change is too rapid.

❑ The personal costs are too high compared to the rewards.

❑ The needs of the work group are ignored.

Ultimate objectives often are not well defined, even to managers and supervisors, and no transitional guidelines are provided. The workforce is often downsized with the promise that the work left behind will soon be eliminated, but no plans to do so are visible. Work slows down and complaints begin.

BRIDGE THE GAP

The manager has to work harder than ever before to set a climate for effective performance in a changing environment. To provide an atmosphere in which employees can find definitions of their work, the organization's goals, a future they can believe in, and direction for their own career will require a focusing of employee efforts. You can begin this process by concentrating employee concerns on their work group and what it should be doing. Begin by:

- Thinking through and articulating for yourself where the group is going in terms of what you believe to be organizational objectives. Specifically, what will be the role of the group and what will it look like after the change is implemented?

- Sharing that vision with employees and talking through their concerns.

- Asking employees to join you in designing a bridge that will take the group from where it is now to where employees envision it being. Identify tasks that will have to be performed and obstacles that will have to be overcome. Set meaningful goals.

Use the techniques described in this book to determine how tasks and responsibilities can be defined and delegated to individuals for accomplishment. Schedule periodic meetings to permit employees to share individual progress and pool ideas to facilitate the change process. You can transform unfocused, uninformed, non-participating, complaining, anxious employees into responsible stakeholders once they realize they can make a direct contribution to the organization's transition.

CASE STUDY 6

Implementing Change

Terence is the purchasing manager for New Concepts, a medium-size computer software company. Senior management announced last week that the company was restructuring to cut costs and improve its standing in the marketplace. Some workers will be laid off and a number of changes will be made in internal and external procedures pertaining to production, sales, and the acquisition of materials and supplies.

The changes were a complete surprise to Terence and other managers at his level, who had not been consulted. Specific goals are very sketchy but Terence has determined that he will have to reduce the cost of supplies and materials by 15% and reduce his departmental operating budget by 10%. Guidelines for this transition have not been provided.

Purchasing employees were stunned by the announcement and the lack of concrete information concerning the changes. Many are worried about their status when the layoff occurs and others worry that their careers are going down the tubes. Productivity comes to a standstill as employees become more negative and devote their time to commiserating with each other.

Terence is also concerned for himself and his future. It is obvious that the organization cannot tolerate the drain on productivity and the negative attitudes being displayed. He wants to turn the group around, but is not sure how. What would you do?

_____

_____

_____

_____

_____

_____

_____

_____

Turn to page 86 and check your ideas with those of the author.

PART

IX

Review and Commitment to the Future

CONGRATULATIONS!

You have completed the activities and exercises in this book. It's time now to measure your progress. Which of the statements on the following two pages are true and which are false?

REVIEW

Answer the following true/false questions.

True   **False**

_____   _____   1. Most managers excel at delegation.

_____   _____   2. Delegation is an indispensable management skill.

_____   _____   3. It's all right to delegate tasks you dislike.

_____   _____   4. Delegation is essential to the development of employees and the improvement of productivity.

_____   _____   5. Employees appreciate your intervention in their decision making.

_____   _____   6. The list of tasks a manager cannot delegate is quite long.

_____   _____   7. Employees dislike managers who delegate.

_____   _____   8. As you move up, you must learn to delegate operating tasks you once performed yourself.

_____   _____   9. Delegation is one way to use and reinforce creative talents.

_____   _____   10. Managers must always keep key results areas in mind when delegating.

_____   _____   11. Delegation is a positive act and requires very little thought or preparation.

_____   _____   12. You don't really know what people can do until you give them a chance under the proper conditions.

_____   _____   13. Secretaries and administrative assistants should be restricted to word processing, filing, and answering phones.

_____   _____   14. The heart of the delegation process is the interaction between the supervisor and the employee when the assignment is communicated.

_____ _____ 15. A common management mistake is failing to delegate authority commensurate with the task.

_____ _____ 16. The goal in delegation is the satisfactory completion of the assigned task through the personal efforts of those assigned the task.

_____ _____ 17. Teaching employees to solve problems helps prepare them for delegation.

_____ _____ 18. Any time you perform a task someone else could do, you keep yourself from a task only you can do.

Check your answers with the author's on the next page.

REVIEW ANSWERS

1. False. Name five in your circle of acquaintances.

2. True. If you are not delegating, you are not managing.

3. True. Chances are very good you will find someone who enjoys them. We usually don't do very well what we dislike.

4. True. Try it, you'll like the results.

5. False. Do you like it?

6. False. Make a list. You will be amazed how short it is (if you are honest).

7. False. Research reflects just the opposite.

8. True. If you don't, your upward progress will stop or you will burn out.

9. True. If you don't delegate, creativity will die.

10. True. Accomplishing results in key results areas is what your job is all about.

11. False. Thought and preparation assure success.

12. True. Everyone needs a chance to show what they can do.

13. False. They are usually capable of much, much more.

14. True. This is the critical connection.

15. True. Too often it is all or nothing.

16. True. Too much interference spoils the results.

17. True. It will make your life much easier.

18. True. And don't you forget it!

TEN TRAPS TO AVOID

Avoid the ten traps listed on the next page.

TEN TRAPS TO AVOID

Check those you intend to avoid.

- ❏ 1. Thinking you can do everything yourself.

- ❏ 2. Failing to give employees challenging assignments with enough latitude to handle them.

- ❏ 3. Careless selection of an authority level when assigning a project.

- ❏ 4. Overlooking delegation opportunities for untried and untested employees.

- ❏ 5. Holding on to non-management tasks that someone else could do.

- ❏ 6. Too little or too much follow-up.

- ❏ 7. Withholding vital information pertinent to a delegated assignment.

- ❏ 8. Failure to recognize employee accomplishments.

- ❏ 9. Overburdening your best, most trusted people because you have not prepared anyone else.

- ❏ 10. Failing to hold a critique with an employee after the accomplishment of a major task to see what you both have learned.

A DELEGATION CHECKLIST

The following checklist is designed to guide the manager through the delegation process.

1. **PERSONAL PREPARATION**

   I have reviewed my job and analyzed or identified:

   _____ my duties and responsibilities
   _____ key results areas
   _____ objectives
   _____ management tasks versus operating work
   _____ the assignments I can delegate

2. **PLANNING THE DELEGATION**

   I have planned the delegation and established or considered:

   _____ the objectives to be accomplished
   _____ completion dates
   _____ standards to be met
   _____ the decision making required
   _____ the amount of authority to be delegated
   _____ budget and other resource requirements
   _____ how involved I want to be
   _____ what feedback I want and when I want it
   _____ the person to whom I will delegate

3. **SELECTING THE RIGHT PERSON**

   I have selected an employee after considering:

   _____ to whom the work logically belongs
   _____ who has the interest or the ability
   _____ who will find the work challenging
   _____ whom the assignment will help to develop
   _____ who has been overlooked in the past
   _____ who is best qualified
   _____ who has the time
   _____ who will do the best job

4. MAKING THE DELEGATION

When I communicate the delegation I will:

_____ describe the task and the results expected
_____ agree on standards of performance and timetables
_____ determine training needs and when training will be provided
_____ state the amount and frequency of feedback I expect
_____ define parameters and resources, including budgets
_____ spell out the level of authority
_____ tell others who is in charge

5. FOLLOWING THROUGH

I will follow through by:

_____ setting reasonable reporting and review schedules
_____ respecting the level of delegation given
_____ communicating freely and openly
_____ supporting the employee to the extent required
_____ offering encouragement and reinforcing employee strengths and abilities
_____ recognizing achievement
_____ intervening only if *absolutely* necessary

DEVELOP A PERSONAL ACTION PLAN

Think over the material you have read. Review the self-analysis questionnaires and the Missed Opportunities page. Rethink the case studies and the reinforcement exercises. What have you learned about delegation? What have you learned about yourself as a delegator? How can you apply what you have learned? Make a commitment to yourself to become a better delegator and a more effective manager by designing a personal action plan to help you accomplish this goal.

The following guide may help you clarify your goals and outline the actions required to achieve them.

1. My current delegation skills are effective in the following areas:

_____

_____

2. I need to improve my delegation skills in the following areas:

_____

_____

3. My goals for improving my delegation skills are as follows (be sure they are specific, attainable, and measurable):

_____

_____

4. These people are resources who can help me achieve my goals:

_____

_____

5. Following are my action steps, along with a timetable to accomplish each goal:

_____

_____

RESPONSES TO CASE STUDIES

Case Study 1: The Do-It-Yourself Manager

Joanne's supervisor didn't waste time getting to the point. She simply asked her to talk about her workload and that of her subordinates. The contrast made the problem obvious. When Joanne explained her rationale, the supervisor would not buy it. She suggested that Joanne take a good look at her subordinates and their past work record. Most were high achievers when given the chance. She suggested that Joanne was afraid to let go of responsibility and authority and perhaps enjoyed "doing" work more than "managing" work. Joanne then admitted that perhaps she didn't know how to let go and still maintain control. The discussion concluded with Joanne agreeing to attend a seminar on delegating and to work closely with her supervisor when she was unsure of how to proceed.

Case Study 2: Baffled by the Budget

Jordan has to release total control of the budget process in his unit in order to get operating control. He should make key staff members responsible for their part of the budget and hold them accountable for results. This means they should participate in the development of the budget and its day-to-day administration.

Jordan's administrative assistant could be assigned responsibility for pulling together the tentative budget with the help and input of the section heads. When they feel it is complete, they can present it to Jordan for review and approval and then follow up to see that everyone stays on track.

RESPONSES TO CASE STUDIES (continued)

Case Study 3: Making Choices

It is good that Olivia has identified Mary Wong's strengths and is delegating to her. She may be delegating so much, however, that Mary is carrying an unfair share of the load and other employees are being prevented from learning new things. Balancing tasks among employees is always difficult, especially when there are one or two you know can do it all and the others would be a risk. You can minimize the risk when assigning work to employees you don't know well by planning the delegation carefully, following up on progress frequently, and training as necessary. Otherwise, you and your "Mary Wongs" will be doing all the important and complex work yourselves and your other employees will be stagnating.

Case Study 4: The Incomplete Data Dilemma

Like many managers, Marla is delegating sufficient authority to capable people to get the work done. Unfortunately, she is not making it clear to everyone involved who is in charge of the investigations, and much of the data input is to her instead of to the employee in charge of the project. In spite of her efforts to translate the information and pass it on quickly, she has become a communications block. Her "translations" may not be accurate, and her intervention prevents the employee who needs the data from asking clarifying questions or requesting additional information. Her employees become defensive when she criticizes them for not handling information well because she is the reason and they are reluctant to say so.

Case Study 5: The Delegation Disaster

Gino is to be commended for realizing the need to delegate, but he moved too quickly and without preparing the people properly.

Gino should have taken the time to get to know each person and to learn something about their needs, abilities, and goals. It would also have been helpful to share his management style and personal goals for the organization. A gradual increase in delegated tasks with employees participating in determining the authority level would have been less threatening to the employees, since they did not seem to understand delegation or have confidence in their ability to undertake new assignments.

Case Study 6: Implementing Change

The first thing Terence needs is to get his own act together. He should seek out as much information as possible about the organization's goals and how they are expected to be achieved. Terence should start by talking to his own boss about the transition. Terence should go into that meeting with a list of questions about implementing the changes and the amount of authority he has for action. From what he learns and from what he already knows about the department, he should be able to articulate a reasonable vision of where the group is going. He is now in a position to share this vision with employees and answer at least some of their questions. Terence and the group can then begin to plan how the change objectives for purchasing can be accomplished, i.e., how can the cost of materials and supplies be reduced by 15%? What are some ways the departmental operating budget can be cut by 10%? Tasks and responsibility can be assigned and timetables set. In so doing, the group will have moved from a demoralized, negative state to one of understanding and positive action.

NOTES

NOTES

NOTES